GO NOW

Encouragement For Your Journey

T.B. LaBerge

Copyright © 2019 Todd B. LaBerge
All rights reserved.

Edited by Mark Hannah & Helen Simmons

Cover and interior design
by Allison LaBerge

CONTENTS

	Forward	*v*
	Acknowledgments	*vii*
	Author's Notes	*ix*
1	Hold On	1
2	Have Faith	101
3	Love Always	331
	About the Author	413

To my lovely wife,

who helps me to love fiercely and humbly,
who teaches me patience and kindness.
I love you Allie.

FORWARD

By J.S. Park

I first met Todd online.

I should say that I met him through his writings. He wrote a lot about love. The sort of stuff that might make you roll your eyes a bit. But Todd wrote the stuff like he meant it. He really did. When I finally met Todd in person, I knew that he was the real deal. He had love written all over him. The day I met him, I had this very strange haircut and he didn't even mention it. We had Korean BBQ and he was serving me and my wife the whole time. He was so nice to us that I was turning red. It was not an act for Todd; he hardly thought twice about refilling our drinks. We had a waiter but he insisted.

One thing that surprised me about Todd was his humor. I couldn't stop laughing around him. Every third sentence was a razor-sharp quip, and every fifth sentence he was thanking Jesus for something. You would think this would get annoying, like a very spiritual Marvel movie, but it wasn't. I felt a lot lighter around Todd. He's the kind of guy you could laugh with all day long, and then you felt safe enough to tell him the hardest stuff about you, and he would stay.

I met Allie online, too. I should say, I met Allie when she and Todd asked me to officiate their wedding. I began premarital counseling for her and Todd. Even through a laptop screen, Allie was a wondrous wave of laughter and lightness. I gave Todd a look: I get it, brother. I could see immediately why they were attracted to each other: they already had the ocean-deep old-couple love.

They had been together for a thousand years. They were two cute oak trees finding comfort in the other's shade. They were natural.

Todd and Allie told me that their life goal was to bring flowers to a world bereft of beauty. They had read that somewhere. I can tell you that their goal did not remain merely book knowledge. Their way of being in the world could plant whole gardens. They have that Resurrection energy.

On their wedding day, I was going through some things. They didn't know it then, but they helped me get through those things. I think there will be some encouragement in this book that will help you get through some things, too. They love you like they love me, dear reader: purely, completely, wholly, and with all the laughter in the world.

Thank you, Todd and Allie. And grace and peace be with you, fellow reader.

ACKNOWLEDGMENTS

A special thank you to:

My beautiful wife who deserves every kiss, vacation, and chocolate milkshake in the world for helping me design & layout this book, Mark Hannah & Helen Simmons for their impeccable skills of proofreading, and Joon Park who encouraged me to write this book and continues to do so with his kind words and friendship.

AUTHOR'S NOTES

Dear Reader,

I want to thank you for taking the time to read through this labor of love, it means more than you'll ever know.

In this day and age, it seems that we are bombarded by anger. Everything is happening at once, every idea we have is being held at extremes. We have lost the importance and value of being silent and still. Life, it becomes exhausting. This book is for those who are weary of life, of the pressures to always be right and perfect. Those who are weary of responsibilities and our own self-worth in what we bring. This book is meant to lift up, encourage and enlighten, to speak to the parts of our hearts that ache with loneliness and a desire to be seen.

I hope you are lifted up, both in mind, body, and spirit. I'm here to tell you that it's okay to rest, to lay down and be recharged. You have a long journey ahead of you, take the time to recover and refill. May the words that are written on these pages be ones of growth and healing, of encouragement and hope. Perhaps, by the end of these pages, you will seek out those around you, to love and help. Rest now, weary traveler.

-T.B. LaBerge

HOLD ON

It all takes time, but it
takes us to a place we
never thought we'd go,
a land of strength
and beauty.

When your heart hurts and it all seems so overwhelming, go now to the throne room of God, find Him waiting for you with arms wide open. Only in the arms of Christ can we find shelter; only in the arms of Christ can we find our worth. The world is hard, but God is good, and when we do this life with Him, we find the path worth traveling. Rest in Him, be renewed in Him, and allow His joy to become your joy; because He longs for you to return again to Him, in the only place that love is born.

When winter has beaten
the world into the ground,
the day comes when the sun
rises, the earth starts to thaw,
and the flower makes its way
to the surface. No matter
what sorrow you have gone
through, you will rise again
more beautiful than ever.

Fear drives most of our lives. It disguises itself in our anger, pride, and selfishness.

Learn to see where your fear manifests itself, then have the courage to lay it down and choose love.

Pain is not beautiful.
It is the healing that takes
place afterwards, which
results in something
wonderful, though we
may not always realize it.

There is a profound courage shown when we can love again, even in the face of pain and sorrow, like a flower that reaches for the sun, even after it endured the harshness of winter.

Healing calls for patience, but it also calls for a brave heart because when you have healed fully, you will learn to love each day that you are alive.

The pain may never make sense, but the thing to remember is that you survived, and that is reason enough to move on.

You can reach out or you can curl up in a ball sobbing away. Either way, God is quick to be there with you. He has a way of finding us in our need, and we always need Him.

You'll have moments when you feel like a lion, and moments when you feel like a mouse. Just know that no matter how you feel, you still have a heartbeat and a soul worthy of love. So learn to roar even when you feel small, because you are more than the feelings you may have.

The ache of wishes not fulfilled can consume you if you think that life is about your expectations. Don't you know that life is more than plans not achieved? Life is so much bigger than that Life is meant to be lived, not just planned. Let go, love and give yourself room to grow. That ache does not define you.

You are seen, known, and heard. You have a worth far beyond what this world has told you, for you are loved. From morning till night, you are loved.

A tender heart can create beautiful things, and when we have something as precious as a big heart we open a door that many people long to find. Be willing to allow your heart to reach borders that are closed, because when we let Christ speak through the door that has been unlocked, we can welcome weary travelers home.

Beauty is found in each morning we have to begin again, the opportunity to try once more with new possibilities.

Sometimes we bleed from
the memories others leave,
and sometimes we bleed
for the memories we wish
others would have left.
Either way, do not dwell
on what was never meant.
Live the moments you have
and learn to love the life
that is in front of you.

One day, when you have crossed that mountain of sorrow, you will see the valley before you and the sun will rise. In that moment, you will know that you have survived a broken heart. You will be different, you will be someone else completely, but you will be alive and well. The next step is to learn what it all means- joy, love, life; it's all waiting for you.

Your present sadness must not dictate your future joy. Hold on, for tomorrow brings something new.

With shattered hearts we learn to live, with empty hands we reach for hope, and with hollowed eyes we seek beauty. No one is entitled to be perfect in order to live. We begin the moment we step out and choose to move forward.

The words you say carry more weight than you know, and to some, they may weigh more than they can handle. Be kind, speak with purpose and clarity, always with the intent to help those around you grow. If you do say words that are hurtful, be quick to use words that heal, and in doing this you will find that you are being more and more like Christ; speaking truth in love.

Heartbreak is not the end of your story, we do not end this journey with tears, they will be wiped away and you will know love unending. Hold on, your pain matters, and your joy will be infinite because our home is not found in the valley of the shadow of death, our home is found in a land far greater than what we've known.

In the late hours of the night, you are overcome with emotions that you cannot explain. Fear not, you are not alone. Sometimes we feel deeply because the silence is trying to speak words that can only be felt. Listen, learn, and live. You might need to help someone learn these same lessons someday.

Yes, you've cried all night, but still, your heart beats; There is hope in heartbreak, beauty in pain, and life in the aftermath.

Perseverance is placing one foot in front of the other, even if it drags.

Confusion is never a finality. You can, and you will continue. Just because it doesn't make sense now, doesn't mean you will always be left alone and wondering. Have courage, you are going to be fine.

You want community?
Be community.

You want love? Be loving to others.

You want friendship? Be a friend.

You want something more?
Be something more.

Sometimes the things we want
most in life, start when we are the
first to initiate it, so go out and be.

One does not see who they are in the shadow of night, it is only in the warmth of the sun that we see who we really are. Just because you feel cold and alone in this season of life, it does not mean that the sun will never rise again. Beloved, it's darkest before the dawn, so hold on, you will feel the warmth of love once again.

You thought you had it figured out, and maybe you did, maybe you were happy and feeling alive. Now it's all gone, and you are left wondering "Why did I go through that?" and it begins to hurt, like a weight on your chest. Just know, that's how life is sometimes; you have sweet and wonderful moments, moments full of endless possibilities and joy. But then you have moments that are deeply wounding, and you have to teach yourself to keep going. That sometimes you fall, but you will always have the choice to get back up, and love what you have; even if it's only a heartbeat.

Patience, dear heart.
Let your joy be true and your
consistency speak of love.
You shall have your moment in
the sun, with spring and flowers
and a soul to share it with. But all
flowers need the water of winters'
snow to be able to fully bloom.

You'll have days where
sadness sets its teeth in,
and you can do nothing but
breathe sad breaths, sigh sad
sighs, and cry sad tears.
It's okay, it's okay to lay
down and let that sadness
wash over you, just as long
as you learn to keep your
head up; Don't let the
sadness drown you, learn
to float and swim, you'll
find safe ground soon… Just
don't drown, don't give up.

Sorrow is a heavy burden to carry, this is why we must be patient with those who carry it; they will get to where they need to be, just give them time.

Nothing feels quite right, does it? I haven't felt like this in a while, and it hurts to think. When did this fog set in? Where did my lighthouse go? What happened to the things I once was so sure of? It feels hollow, and I'm scared that it won't go back, that I'll drift for a while and not ever have anything to return to.

Oh, but I see now, I must look up and see the beauty of that northern star; the silence of it will not tell me where to go, but the fact that it is where it is, will guide me home.

Do we not all have a northern star? Do we not all have Christ?

Who He is, and where He is, is the sign for where we must go; that is hope in the darkness, in the confusion of it all. Christ standing with arms out stretched, showing us our way home, showing us our way to Him.

Dream dreams that keep you awake.

Thank God we are called by Jesus to pray and love our enemies; because we all are someone's enemy.

The thing to always remember
is that there is someone greater
than all the worries at hand,
for only one person has defeated
death; that is something that
should give us an abundance
of joy and peace.

Joy will outlast sorrow.

Courageous hearts are
often covered in scars.

Press on! When the world has left you, or when loved ones have gone, press on! Never stop where you are, never give up, be relentless in your journey. Press on, dear heart, for courage will only fail when you have chosen to surrender. Continue on and know that you will see fairer days.

I love this place, the ruins of my failure,
and I think that's the problem.
I'm clinging onto something that is
gone, that has left and will never return.
It's time I moved on, found a place that
is no longer ash and fire, let it be that
I find a place that is solid, that holds
new memories of love and hope.
Let me set sail to a shore that is far
greater than anything that I have left
behind, for these scars will never heal
if I do not get to a safe place. I seek the
shadow of a better place, so that I can
escape the same sun that has burned me
so many times before, I'm looking for a
place that I can dry my eyes and rest my
soul. I am looking for that place that
cannot be found here, I am looking
for that person that has been calling
my name. And so, I leave, this place
that I once called home, for a new
land that is all my own.

Don't break my heart by
saying you've given up,
please continue to fight.

We often forget that our hearts
beat to keep us alive,
not to keep us down.

Hail the heart that sees stars
when storms are present.

Hail the mind that chooses
to love instead of hate.

Hail the soul that serves
instead of choosing to rule.

Have the courage to be humble.

It is far easier to pat someone's head,
encourage them, and then send them
on their way, than it is to sit
in silence with them. It is up to us
to choose who we are going to be;
are we someone who is a pit stop?
Or someone who walks along
with others, never letting them
travel the journey alone.

These moments are like snowflakes; it's best to build something beautiful before it all melts with the beginning of a new season.

You will know more
failures than victories.
The key is to remember
the victories when the
failures seem to overcome
everything else.

When we are tempted by that voice in our heads, telling us that we are unworthy and unloved, that our pain is not worth dealing with. You tell that voice to look at the cross and flee, because the cross does not show us that our pain is insignificant, rather, it shows us that our pain is significant enough for a God to come and suffer with us.

It's okay not to have all
the answers; you don't
owe that to anyone.

How cruel it is to have souls that cannot be explained in words; but how lovely it is to be able to feel such emotions. It is a beautiful paradox.

Take your sadness, all of your pain and make it into art; paint something magnificent, so that when you look back on it, you can remember that your sadness can be beautiful.

How fragile we treat the world;
who has become so hard.

HAVE FAITH

You wanted love so desperately that you forgot that love is patient, and now you're broken-hearted with a world full of regrets.

Have heart beloved! Christ's love is patient, and He is not prideful, return to Him and find that love that you have craved for so long.

To love at all, I must love
God first. To love deeper,
I must love God deepest.
To be good in my love,
I must allow the goodness
of God to be first and
foremost. I cannot love
from myself, only in and
through God can I ever
hope to help grow that
which I love and cherish.

Jesus cried "It is finished!" so why don't we? Why are we not living in that proclamation? Beloved, you are loved and set free, the veil is torn, and you are allowed to go in Christ's power to all the corners of this world. Do not let anything in this life keep you from remembering Jesus' cry from the cross.

The same voice that brought the stars into existence, speaks your name with love and truth. Will you not love that voice more than the beauty of the night sky? Will you not gaze upon the Creator as you would the very heavens He made? Will you not answer His call?

I need love that I do not deserve, grace that I have not earned, and forgiveness that I have not sought.

I need it and I need it and I need it till the end.

So many times, I need God
to destroy my idea of Him,
just so that I can love Him
more; it is a scary thing,
but a beautiful thing.

More than anything, I need Jesus; let me never forget a single moment of that truth, because He is the only one who will calm storms and revive my soul. I need Him just as I need the air in my lungs, or the warmth of the sun. Jesus Christ is not an accessory to my life, He is my life.

God is present in it all;
whether in times of sorrow
or joy, He is weeping and
rejoicing with us.

You can never go before God and expect to stay the same, He is in the business of transforming and molding, making us new and lovely. If you are to go before God, go with the understanding that you will never be the same, you will be a living hallelujah, beautiful and pleasing to Him.

When you have strayed away from the path, call Jesus. When you have betrayed his trust, call Jesus. When you have become something unrecognizable, call Jesus. He will always answer, for He is in the business of saving those who need it, and we are all desperately in need of a Savior.

Go to Jesus, whatever it is that is on your heart, take it to the one who knows your heart. Let Him be the constant in this world of inconsistencies; let Christ be the rock that you build your life on, because He is the only foundation that will stand in the season of pain. He is all that we need, so return to Him, and be restored.

Your heart hurts and it all seems so overwhelming, go now to the throne room of God, find Him waiting for you with arms wide open. Only in the arms of Christ can we find shelter, only in the arms of Christ can we find our worth. The world is hard, but God is good, and when we do this life with Him, we find the path worth traveling.

Rest in Him, be renewed in Him, and allow His joy to become your joy; because He longs for you to return again to Him, in the only place that love is born.

I'm gonna pray, and sing, and hope; I'm gonna weep, and beg, and moan; I'm gonna fight, and struggle, and doubt. But in the end, I'm gonna be His and He is gonna be mine. For my life is not my own, but the product of a God who breathed life into dust and said, "Follow Me, out into the storm." and if I fall, He is quick to answer, for He is the God who calms the storms, and He is the God who is with us in it all.

If you are low today, look to Jesus. If you are filled with shame and guilt, look to Jesus. If your heart sings of joy, look to Jesus. If fear be dormant in your soul, look to Jesus. If you have lungs with air and a heart that beats, look to Jesus. For only in Him, is there an everlasting refuge to be found.

We all have growth that needs to be done in our lives, but as long as Christ is leading us; we shall bloom all the more.

I am cruel, I am apathetic,
I am broken, and I am
always falling short;
therefore I must point
everyone I know to Christ,
He is consistent in a world
full of inconsistencies,
He is faithful when all
the world is unfaithful,
and He is good when
goodness cannot be found.

The victory on the cross will always out-weigh the defeat in our hearts, Christ cried "It is finished!" It is up to us to live in that proclamation.

Why do we love the flower when we are loved by the Gardener? Why do we love the shadow when the sun shines brightly upon us? Jesus has offered Himself to us, so why do we choose the world? We must be willing to let Christ mold us and change us, teaching our hearts to love the Gardener who makes us beautiful, and the sun who gives us life. For, in the end, it is Jesus.

I am weak, but Christ
is strong; and today,
just as every day, I
need Him to carry me.

There is a joy in the knowledge
that we can pour out all that
we need to say to God, and He
will be patient in our ramblings.
Then, once all has been said, He
holds us in His arms, reassuring
that we are free to be open with
Him and to lay our fear down.
He makes us new by simply
listening to us, and then
shaping us in the silence.

The real cry of all our hearts is that we need Jesus, that we need Him to restore us, to fill us, to love us, and to never leave us. Beloved, He will always answer our cries, and He will even hear our whispers; always responding with love and grace.

Go to Jesus, whatever it is that is on your heart, take it to the one who knows your heart. Let Him be the constant in this world of inconsistencies; let Christ be the rock that you build your life on, because He is the only foundation that will stand in the season of pain. He is all that we need, so return to Him, and be restored.

A man who focuses on
the dark, when holding a
lantern, instead of what
the light provides, is
bound to trip and fall.
We must not look into
the corners of darkness
when we have the light of
truth in our lives, for we
are called into the light of
God and that is the only
source that will guide us,
and others, home.

How wonderful it is
to see the night sky,
full and radiant with stars
that were put there by
the greatest Artist of all
creation. How wonderful
it is to see all nature and
know that the Author of
it all knows us by name
and calls us beloved.

Within the three days that
Christ was in the grave;
The world mourned, Heaven
prepared a throne-room for
the Eternal King of Glory,
and hell witnessed the
collapse of its empire.

Sometimes in the silence
and sorrow of life, Christ
is doing His greatest work.

Apathy kills the heart's call for God, it silences our desire to seek Christ and all that he provides. Pray now that God would deliver you of your apathetic spirit before it drags you away from the only heart that truly loves you.

I looked across the expanse
of my shame, the ocean of
disobedience, Christ took my
hands and said "This is not
for you to see, look to Me."
I did, and I was made new.

If we are amazed by the stars
and all the wonders of nature,
can we not also be moved to
tears by the grand composition
that God is doing to us?

In our heartbreak;
Christ finds His way
through the cracks.

Oddly enough, it's the storms that whisper His name, the storms that make His presence most known. So, prepare yourself when the seas of life begin to grow restless, because you might be getting ready to encounter God; what a heartbreakingly beautiful thing it is to behold.

I hope that at the heart of whatever you are looking for; you find Jesus there.

When your heart is a mess
and it has found its way
astray, send it home,
send it to Christ. Let it
live with Him and know
that no matter how far
we have wandered; He is
always with us guiding
us back to where we are
supposed to be, which is
in His everlasting arms.

Sin tries to convince us that Christ remembers every mistake we make; Grace tells us that Christ remembers every tear we shed.

The reality is that Jesus will wipe away both.

May we always look to Christ
for our security and not just
the future, for it is in Christ
alone that we can ever find true
hope, love, grace, and peace.
Only Jesus looks at us and
tells us to follow him, nothing
else will ever beckon you to
something eternal and good.

Our pursuit of God will lead us to the place our hearts have been searching for since birth, home.

God is always present. Even when it seems like all is silent and lonesome, He is present; loving you like only He can.

When I am plagued by doubts,
let my heart go to Christ.

When I feel inadequate,
let me understand my worth in Jesus.

When I have moments of weakness,
let my strength come only from
Emmanuel.

When I rise and when I sleep,
let it always be about Jesus.

When it comes to anything,
let it always lead me to Christ.

Pray in sorrow, pray in anger, pray in joy; pray, pray, pray. Pray until Heaven responds, and the Earth is restored to holiness; Pray until Christ wipes away our tears and puts to death sin once and for all.

Rest your wounded and weary heart in Jesus, for He is making all things new.

Take your tears to Christ, for He will wipe them all away.

Submit your troubles to God, for He is the only one who will end all suffering.

Jesus is good, so find Him in the storms as well as in the calm.

When I begin to
feel unloved, I must
remember to look at
Christ; for He is love,
and I cannot deny
what He is in me.

Silence and solitude will never
be the things that define you,
because it is the Creator of
it all that speaks your name
in the moments of desperation.
Weep tonight, for tomorrow
you shall reap joy and know
 a life without wounds or
sorrow; because Christ is
making all things new.

Who whispered that your worth was found in the reflection of a mirror? Oh beloved, do you not know your true worth is found in the reflection of Christ? Let Him whisper His love, let Him guide you back home.

The Christian's response to doubt (as it should be to everything), must be love. Your brother may be struggling with sin, you must support him by radiating the love of Christ. Your sister is plagued with guilt, speak Christ's love and it will soothe the storm that rages within her. In all things, show love.

Whoever has your heart,
has your future, this is
why we must give it over
to Christ; because He is
the only one who knows
what the next step will be.

In the sight of man, I will be forgotten; but in the eyes of God, I will never fade. There is a joy that out lasts sorrow, a love that grows stronger than hate, and there is a hope that will restore the hopeless. Christ is that, He is all that we need, and He desires us. I shall rejoice in this truth, and I shall let it grow ever more within my soul.

When was the last time you let God's grace be enough? When did you allow Him to be the foundation to everything you do? When did you let Christ bind your wounds and kiss your scars? Until you have let Him be all that you live for; you will always be looking for something to live for.

Death was our old sentence,
but Christ says that life is
our new story; and that's
a story that needs to be
read aloud, and often.

I want God, in my weakness, in my pain, in my joy, in my strength, in my apathy, in my love, and in my life. I want God so completely; that everything that I do is covered in His Spirit.

Do our hearts truly hunger after God? Or do we simply tell our hearts to hunger after God. Either way, we must never stop seeking after Him; because He will have us, whether we want Him or not. One day, we will wake up with the desire to seek Him and realize that the longing that we thought the world would satisfy is slowly being satisfied only by Christ.

The victory of the Cross is not
simply ripples in a lake and we are
feeling the last few waves of it;
It is the lake. It is what we now
live in. We are all given a choice
to swim in grace, or suffocate
on land, because we think we
can do better on our own.

Jesus is finely tuning us in our doubts, for when we feel no song of praise coming from our lips, it is because Christ is tuning you to the melody of Heaven. Music and praise will burst forth once again, just let the Master pull and tighten the areas of your life that have gone slack. He is preparing you for a grand concert in which you will be used for the glory of God.

We criticize ourselves for being weak when it comes to our faith, but isn't that the whole point? We are weak, but He is strong. Isn't that why we are here in the first place? Because we needed a Father to carry us once again, until we have reached our homeland.

We all reach for things that can never be; yet, the One thing that should never have been, reaches down to us. Christ invites us to partake in His love, the same love that all of creation groans for, the same love that conquered death and brought about the stars; this love is reaching down to us, and He calls us beloved.

Think yourself not small, beloved; rather, think Him bigger than yourself.

Take your wounds to Christ,
for He knew all the hurt
a soul can endure,
and still He loved.

Find me where my heart lies;
and may it always be found
in the arms of Christ.

Jesus is so present, even when we don't feel like He is or even when we are not present ourselves; Christ is still there.

God speaks an infinite amount of truths. Should we not at least echo them?

God created the universe with His life giving breath; Jesus saved the whole of creation with His final breath. It seems only fitting that we be willing to praise Him with all the breath we can give.

Do we fight for the hearts
of men or do we fight
for the heart of God?
Whichever heart you seek,
know that one will destroy
and the other will restore.

If the love of God is
not enough for you, then
I would suggest that you
are not experiencing the
love of God; because it is a
love that overflows, and no
sane man can ever deny the
abundance of a full cup.

Our need for God will always be greater than our want for Him. When we are in those seasons, we must let the need for God devour our desire for Him. It is in that moment that we start to hunger and thirst again. That is when we see the glory of His unending love. That is when we can begin to be children of God, loving and obeying faithfully.

How odd that we think
the hands that disobeyed
are the same hands that
can save, and the hands
that saved are the same
hands that wound us.
Jesus does not reject us.
He still holds out His
beautiful hands for us to
hold and be renewed.
This is grace; that we were
lost and now we are saved.

The fact that Jesus commands my destiny is the greatest relief and joy in all of creation.
We cannot do any good apart from God, and when we try to hold onto the reins of life, we end up losing all control.
Surrender, receive, rejoice, give, and repeat!

Past mistakes do not dictate future joy. Only when you allow the past to be a part of the present do you lose the joys of tomorrow. Surrender those mistakes to Christ and know that His love for you is not based on your own perfection, but rather on His.

Should we not cling to God's grace? Is it not more faithful than anything this world has to offer? I should hope that my life be found in the everlasting hope of Christ instead of the temporary promises of the world.

Jesus, He is everything.

He calls us beloved. Is that not more wonderful than all the praises of man?

Even a King's most precious goblet must be washed. Never think that you are too dirty to be used by God. For in His world, His grace is endless and transformative.

Jesus said let the children come to Him.
You need to know that He was talking to you too.

If you seek happiness, you will always find someone happier than you. If you seek love, you will find someone more in love than you. If you seek to be holy, you will find a much holier God. But that is the thing with the last one; when we find God, He invites us to stay.

Nothing in this life will truly stay with you, but when it comes to God, we find that we were made to be with Him.

Christ mends the brokenhearted,
and there has not been
one unbroken heart in all the
history of the world.

You are more than empty beds and lonely nights; you are not just a heartbeat under bed sheets. You are complex and wonderful, beautiful and brilliant. Please stop allowing the silence to dictate who you are. You are Christ's. The same voice that awoke the world calls you beloved. Never ever forget that.

When we lose sight of Christ; the reality of purity, love, salvation, redemption, obedience, and everything that Christianity tells us to do, will seem impossible. But when we keep our focus on Christ and what He wants, it becomes as natural as breathing. We can never dictate the commands of God; we can only serve obediently to His gentle and most beautiful call.

How many times did Christ call the "sinner" unto Himself? The answer is every time. So why do we have such a hard time thinking that Christ calls us as well, no matter how bad our sins may be? Jesus has not changed His mind toward us. He is constant in all that He does, including calling us His.

Christ wrecks us, holds us and rebuilds us; it is the greatest blessing we can ever hope for.

Nothing cuts deeper than losing the attention of someone you admire, yet once we have shifted all our adoration to Christ, nothing heals more fully. Don't you feel it, beloved? Don't you hear the song of Heaven singing His grace? Don't you see the wounds that bought you? Look up and see that you have the full attention of Christ and be renewed in that glorious revelation.

If I have given my heart
to Christ, then what right
do I have to say what He
should do with it? If I am to
give Him this soul, should
I not be blessed if He wills
to break it and change it? I
should spend no less than
all my days praising Him for
the pain. For when Christ
breaks our hearts, He does it
so that we might be holy as
He is holy. So, praise Him;
even through the pain.

No saint has ever said that prayer was a hindrance to their growth. In fact, prayer is of monumental importance for any growth at all. Therefore, let us always be found in that holy place: on our knees before a holy God.

Give me Jesus, give me His love, passion, obedience, strength, humility, joy, wisdom, and faith.

Give me Jesus, in the valley and on the mountain, in life or in death, rain or shine.

Give me Jesus, for I know no higher thing to have.

You fail, but Christ doesn't.
He wants you, no matter
what you think.

Jesus loved, obeyed, and did the Will of the Father, even when attacked. So, remember that the next time you are personally confronted. This life is about Christ! Continue doing the work that is set for you.

Nothing will be hated more than God; and nothing will love more than God.

If we say that we are eager to learn the gospel but not to live it, then we are not eager for the gospel at all. The gospel transforms us, it calls us to be a part of it, and it will use us in radical ways. So, be careful in what you say you are willing to do; because Christ is eager for you to be a part of it and He will move Heaven and Earth for you to join in.

Christ gave up His will so that we would be saved; we give up our will so that Christ will be glorified.

The Christian who does not show patience in the face of opposition will have a hard time carrying their cross. In all things, make it clear that Christ speaks from you and through you, so that all who hear know that the Lord is good.

Our joy does not come
from the abundance
of life, but rather an
abundance of Christ.

If there is one thing
that the Cross shows,
it is that God does not
ignore those who suffer,
because the Cross was a
megaphone to the world,
proclaiming that Jesus is a
God who suffers with us.

The reality of Jesus
will always overshadow
the promise of
personal ideology.

Receive grace,
live in grace, show
grace and repeat.

Jesus is our savior. That means He is not just the winner of one thing, but He has won all things; that includes whatever you are struggling with.

There is never a moment in my life in which I do not need Jesus. I cannot expect to take on the day without Him. Just knowing that His mercies are new every day and His love is steadfast is proof enough that He wants to be with me every day. Therefore, I am in constant need of Christ just as my lungs are in need of air, and
my heart is in need of love. Give me Jesus or give me nothing.

Everything God says
or does will never be
good enough until
Christ is enough for us.

What Jesus did versus what we do is that He died for His enemies, while we just criticize them, even when we say that we love Jesus. Have the courage to love your enemies, because then you will be more like Jesus each and every day.

The Christian mindset
should never be of 'That
person is going to hell'
it should be 'How can I
witness Jesus to them, so
that they don't go to hell'.
Until we really know how
much Jesus longs to see
His flock safely home,
we will just sit by as our
brothers and sisters fling
themselves from the cliff,
and we'll be left having to
answer to the shepherd.

We may be from dust,
but we are filled with the
breath of God, counted
as one of His beloved.
That means more than
anything you tell yourself,
or anyone else tells you.

God will always seem
like a disappointment
when our expectations are
not met, instead of His.
The true glory of God
is that He sent His Son
because He knew what
expectation was needed
to be met, and God's true
mercy is that He allows us
to join in and be a part of
this fulfilled expectation.

We deny God by our actions, yet we accuse Him of being absent when our way has led us down a path of isolation. Have the courage to be humble, for a humble heart will lead you to a gracious God.

The magnitude of my own failures tries to make its way back to me, but whenever that happens, that glorious cross makes its appearance, and the empty tomb abolishes those lies that tell me that I am not enough. For I may not be, but Christ is abundantly more than enough; and He calls me beloved.

Courage to fight, courage to walk away, courage to deal with those impossible things in your life; it is all found in the Man who carried the cross and paid the price, who rolled away the stone and now intercedes for us in front of God. Courage is found in Christ. Seek Him and continue to fight, for victory has been placed in Jesus.

The only thing more beautiful than what was done on the cross is what happened on Easter. It was the final declaration that death was defeated.

All that I was,
was nailed to the cross,
and all that I am,
ascended from the tomb.

You may grow weary
of people always telling
you to stop being so
concerned with falling in
love. But never grow tired
of the cross. That is the
place that a God came
down to show you that
you are loved more
than anyone else can
ever possibly love you.

Did you think yourself unlovable when the world stopped, and the heavens mourned? Did you think yourself ugly when the groom was beaten and spit upon? Did you think yourself unworthy when a God screamed out for us? Did you think of your God when He thought of you?

You may want to run and grow in your relationship with Christ. People may even criticize you for not "growing" in the way you should. But if you are in a season of just madly being in love with Him, or a season of sitting and resting at His feet, then so be it. Jesus is with you, that is all that matters.

Are we giving up things in our life because God tells us to, or because we don't want it? God wants it all, even the things you love so much. For what is innocent can quickly corrupt, and what is good will ultimately be bad when we are not willing to trust it in the hands of the Almighty.

Just as dirt on shoes does not define the traveler, so sin does not define the person. Let your definition begin and end with Christ. It's important to know that all who journey are prone to some dirt on their feet. It's whether or not we are willing that our Lord clean it off.

If you want to seek God,
you will actually take
the steps to seek God.
Results are produced
when action is birthed
from desire. Feed your
desire to chase after God,
and then be prepared to
run full speed after Him.

When I am drowning
in the filth of my own
sin, I am reminded that
Christ walked on water,
calmed the storms and
calls the sinner. Jesus
pulls us from despair
so that His glory may
be known. Won't you
go with Him? Won't
you go with Him to the
mountains and to the
country that has been
waiting for you? Fear
not. He will carry you
and He will guide you.
You need only follow.

When the tears have dried and the heart ache has given way, we will find ourselves not far from a God who has held us in our storm, who has knelt in our grief and stayed with us. When all is said and done, we will find ourselves in a better land, holding the hand of a better man.

Have you heard that plea?
Have you felt it course
through your whole body?
That is the cry our
hearts make to the
One who created us.

How we long to be with
Christ daily, every hour
we plead for Him to take
us; and every hour He
tells us to follow.

It's time to get up
and follow.

To look at Jesus with the absence of God's wrath is to look at Jesus with the absence of His Grace. Jesus' sacrifice cannot go unnoticed; it was the ultimate gift of love to a world devoid of it.

Just beyond the crumbling walls
of your own self-righteousness,
lays the land of Grace. This land
is ruled by a loving King.
He welcomes those who are
willing to leave what they have
come to know as safe and accept
what they have heard as foolish.
In this land, you are made free.
In this land, you are made alive.

LOVE ALWAYS

Love the ones who have been given to you and leave the ones who you left in the past. We have a short time in this world. Let's not waste it on things that are not ours. Love actively, live in humility, and be a person who makes the most of each day we have.

Leave them better than how you found them, or don't leave them. Just make them better, strive every day to make each person you meet a little better than how you found them. With this, we make the world a little brighter than the day before.

Love, true and beautiful
love, it shines beyond
the darkness. It shines
through it and removes it.

You were brave for loving
and you were strong for trying.

Your ability to love
and feel deeply is far
more valuable than you
know. Cherish it and
learn to grow with it.

Love does not always have to be this mountaintop experience, but it does need to be as constant as a mountain – never moving, always steady and willing to stay.

If love is to bloom, I must go with you before the throne room, because only in the presence of Christ can we ever hope for a love that will last.

We want love, we want it to overflow and consume us, to make us something new. The important thing to remember is that we must not let that fire go out, because it's nice to want love, but to keep it alive is what love is all about. To feed the flames of love is to feed the flames of the soul; to pursue and encounter, to cherish and engage, this is the heart of love, this is the heart of life.

Let's be brave in our
love so that we can show
others why love matters,
because important things
take courage to do.

Love starts with a fluttering of thoughts and attraction. We think, "Oh, I could see myself with this person." and then the fluttering stops, and it begins to expand, like your chest is going to burst with all the feelings you hold. Yet, it's simply just that – a feeling. It's when you continue to choose daily, saying "I am with this person, and I love them." So, now you go out of your way to show them that they matter, you go beyond where expanding and fluttering can go, and you go to the deepest part of the sea, and you drop your anchor. This is when you have made your choice. There is no going back now. You have bound yourself to the sea, and she is worth being lost in, because you realize that you always had the love of her in your blood.

Love is absolute;
it holds nothing back.
It speaks, lives, grows,
and pours out. To love,
you must be willing
to surrender your
protection, desires,
passions, and ultimately,
your life. This is why
it hurts so much when
love is not returned,
and this is why you
are transformed
when you love Christ.

Love is far from blind.
In fact, it sees all the little
mistakes we make and
still chooses us because
grace must be a part of
love and love a part of
grace. Grace and love are
transformative, and when
we allow them to engage
in our daily relationships
we are allowing them to do
something beautiful and
good: When we do not
let it transform us, we are
choosing not to love at all.

I hope you have the courage
to pursue someone who is
worth pursuing, and not
someone who is convenient.
Convenience is impatience
disguised as your desires.
You are worth more than
what time has told you.
You are worthy of finding
someone who will wait for
you. Don't settle for what is
easy, settle for what is good.

Sensitive hearts are like
a pond; when you say
or do something, it's
like you have tossed a
rock into the heart of it,
the repercussions go to
every part of the pond.
So be gentle, be kind,
and be loving; for each
action will be felt.

It is good to find someone who will listen to your story and then help you write the rest of it.

The difference between changing someone and helping them grow, is that a plant grows, but it does not stop being a plant. You can't change somebody. That transformation happens when Christ enters the picture. We can only help each other grow. Learn to help others become their full potential and not something that they're not.

You cannot be everything to everyone, but you can be you; so be you, and that will be enough.

You don't know what you want, but you know that you want. Now, where do we go from here? How do we find the object of our wants? Are we to wander aimlessly until we realize that what we have wanted is not something, but someone? Perhaps, when we have searched we will find, in the end, that it was you and I, silent in that moment, eager for it all and still hesitant. I should hope that our souls recognize each other, and we can begin to understand this thing called love. That I can hold you and know your name at last, and the warmth of your tears in my hands as I wipe them away; that I can finally whisper in your ear "I am here, and I love you... I love you, I love you, I love you." and we'll be...

Oh, we'll be.

The wisest men are
not those who read the
"best" books or have the
"greatest" conversations;
they are the ones who
love and love well.

Nothing awakens a soul
like knowing that it
is loved. To be loved,
appreciated, fought
for, and encouraged is
something that our hearts
thirst for; and ultimately
all these things can only
be found in Christ.

One may want to love deeply, but until they understand the depths of love, they will never be willing to jump.

I always thought I was
impossible to love, but
then I saw that it was
possible for a God to live,
die, and rise again because
He loved me.

His grace makes us whole,
His love sets us like stone,
and His mercy renews us
daily. To have found this
love, is to have found
what it means to live.

If your heart bleeds the
need to love, let no one
bandage that wound,
for the world is in
desperate need of it.

Soft may the heart of love sound in a world of harsh responses, but grand is the impact of love when all the world has known is hate.

Eloquence in speech can only take you as far as courage will allow. Stop worrying about what you will say. Just find the courage to actually say something.

Isn't it wonderful? The one love that we don't deserve has been given to us! Yet, isn't it heartbreaking? The one love that we most need we refuse, because of our pride.

A different blood flows in
our veins when the sun
has gone to sleep and
all that we held in silent
suddenly finds a voice,
echoing those desires
that we seem to keep
bottled up, hoping
someone will be
around to hear it.

Awake oh heart! For you have many days to beat still, many lives to love, and many journeys to go on. Do not stop beating, not now, for you have not seen the best that is yet to come, you have not experienced the wonder that is just around the corner. Travel on, beat new life, and know that it is not time to sleep; for the sun is high and the music is beautiful. She is out there, waiting for your soul to awaken her heart from her wintery slumber. She is waiting for your voice to bring new life to her very soul.

It's important to protect your heart, yet it's also important to know when your heart is no longer a fortress but instead a prison. Guard it, don't trap it. You will only know how to do that by the guidance of Christ.

We can hope that someone will love us, but in the end, it must be a conscious choice, on our end, to love someone, to love them well each and every day.

To a broken heart, it is easy to fall in love with even the kindest touch. It is fragile work learning to appreciate the right heart, but truly it is of the utmost importance to find it.

There is an infinite amount
of wealth in treasuring
someone's heart; you
should seek to do it often.

You were loved from the beginning and you will be loved until the end. You may not feel it though. You may have to conquer numerous battles and climb a multitude of mountains. But when you have entered that land, which we all must travel to, you shall feel His love as a new dawn arises and you are freed of your burdens; you shall know that you were loved all along and forever more.

I truly believe that in the heart of joyful souls, lies a fierce loyalty to friendship.

Let her know, every single day, let her know how beautiful and wonderful you think she is.

Let him say it to you, every single day, let him tell you what he thinks of you.

Love the heart that forgives.

Never ask for the chance
to love someone. Love does
not require permission.
It's also important to know
that love does not require
anything in return.
Loving someone is
never easy, but it is always
wonderful when it is
done with a selfless heart.

How easy it is to fall in
love with someone who is
in love, to catch a glimpse
of that which we all desire.
How it stings to know that
we must wait until we are
that person, walking hand in
hand with the reality of love.

Nothing ever truly prepares
you for falling in love;
the same goes for
having a broken heart.

I consider it a triumphant thing when you can continue to love after defeat. No nobler thing than they who raise their head after the battle of love has been lost, for they know that tomorrow dawns a new day and their wounds will heal with the promise of future victory.

ABOUT THE AUTHOR

Todd Benjamin Pierson LaBerge was born to Steve and Judy LaBerge in Illinois on May 4th, 1989.
He is the youngest of four boys, and he has loved reading from an early age due to his home-schooled upbringing. He discovered his love for writing when he joined Tumblr in 2011. There, he quickly began writing what was on his heart and through doing so, he gained a following. He currently lives in Georgia with his lovely wife Allison, where he continues to write and make films at *Brand RED Studios*.

---

www.tblaberge.com
Tumblr: tblaberge.tumblr.com
Facebook: T.B. LaBerge
Instagram: @tblaberge
Twitter: @tblaberge
Vimeo: toddlaberge

Other works by T.B. LaBerge:

Unwritten Letters to You
Available on Amazon.com in paperback & kindle format

Made in the USA
Middletown, DE
11 September 2020